How To Use Token Economy and Point Systems

SECOND EDITION

Teodoro Ayllon

How To Manage Behavior Series

R. Vance Hall
and
Marilyn L. Hall
Series Editors

pro·ed
An International Publisher

8700 Shoal Creek Boulevard
Austin, Texas 78757-6897
800/987-3202 Fax 800/397-7633
www.proedinc.com

© 1999, 1982 by PRO-ED, Inc.
8700 Shoal Creek Boulevard
Austin, Texas 78757-6897
800/897-3202   Fax 800/397-7633
www.proedinc.com

Library of Congress Cataloging-in-Publication Data

Ayllon, Teodoro, 1929–
    How to use token economy and point systems / Teodoro Ayllon—2nd ed.
      p.   cm.
    Prev. ed. published with title: How to set up a token economy.
    ISBN-13: 978-089079794-5 (pbk. : alk. paper)
    ISBN-10: 0-89079-794-3 (pbk. : alk. paper)
    1. Token economy (Psychology)   I. Ayllon, Teodoro, 1929–   How to set up a token economy.   II. Title
RC489.T68A94   1999
153.8'5—dc21   98-35124
                                                     CIP

This book is designed in Palatino and Frutiger.

Art Director: Thomas Barkley
Designer: Jason Crosier

Printed in the United States of America

8 9 10 11 12 13 14 15 16 17   17 16 15 14 13

Contents

Preface to Series

The first edition of the *How To Manage Behavior Series* was launched some 15 years ago in response to a perceived need for teaching aids that could be used by therapists and trainers. The widespread demand for the series has demonstrated the need by therapists and trainers for nontechnical materials for training and treatment aids for parents, teachers, and students. Publication of this revised series includes many updated titles of the original series. In addition, several new titles have been added, largely in response to therapists and trainers who have used the series. A few titles of the original series that proved to be in less demand have been replaced. We hope the new titles will increase the usefulness of the series.

The editors are indebted to Steven Mathews, Vice President of PRO-ED, who was instrumental in the production of the revised series, as was Robert K. Hoyt, Jr. of H & H Enterprises in producing the original version.

These books are designed to teach practitioners, including parents, specific behavioral procedures to use in managing the behaviors of children, students, and other persons whose behavior may be creating disruption or interference at home, at school, or on the job. The books are nontechnical, step-by-step instructional manuals that define the procedure, provide numerous examples, and allow the reader to make oral or written responses.

The exercises in these books are designed to be used under the direction of someone (usually a professional) with a background in the behavioral principles and procedures on which the techniques are based.

The booklets in the series are similar in format but are flexible enough to be adapted to a number of different teaching situations and training environments.

R. Vance Hall, PhD, is Senior Scientist Emeritus of The Bureau of Child Research and Professor Emeritus of Human Development and Family Life and Special Education at the University of Kansas. He was a pioneer in carrying out behavioral research in classrooms and in homes. Marilyn L. Hall, EdD, taught and carried out research in regular and special public school classrooms. While at the University of Kansas, she developed programs for training parents to use systematic behavior change procedures and was a successful behavior therapist specializing in child management and marriage relationships.

As always, we invite your comments, suggestions, and questions. We are always happy to hear of your successes in changing your own behaviors and the behaviors of other persons to make your lives more pleasant, productive, and purposeful.

R. Vance Hall &
Marilyn L. Hall
Series Editors

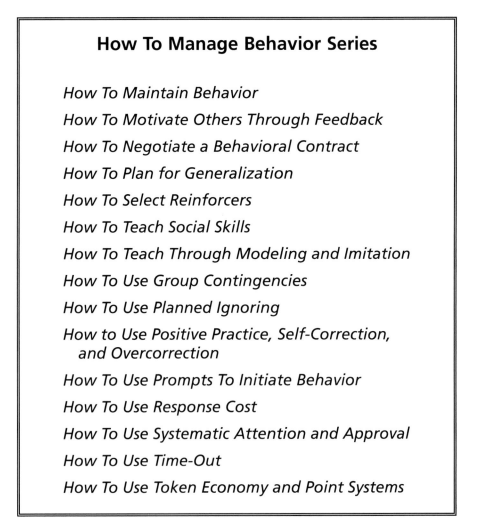

How To Manage Behavior Series

How To Maintain Behavior

How To Motivate Others Through Feedback

How To Negotiate a Behavioral Contract

How To Plan for Generalization

How To Select Reinforcers

How To Teach Social Skills

How To Teach Through Modeling and Imitation

How To Use Group Contingencies

How To Use Planned Ignoring

How to Use Positive Practice, Self-Correction, and Overcorrection

How To Use Prompts To Initiate Behavior

How To Use Response Cost

How To Use Systematic Attention and Approval

How To Use Time-Out

How To Use Token Economy and Point Systems

Introduction

In 1961, I began seven years of exciting collaborative work with Nate Azrin at Anna State Hospital in Anna, Illinois, where we established the first programmatic research on a motivational system for therapy and rehabilitation. Our studies introduced the basic procedures related to behavioral influence through token reinforcement.

At the outset, we specified the conditions under which a token or point system would work or fail. These procedures are now routinely taught and are widely used by parents, teachers, nurses, attendants, aides, and other professionals and paraprofessionals who are responsible for managing and teaching appropriate behavior. *The Token Economy: A Motivational System for Therapy and Rehabilitation,* published in 1968, stands today as the empirical base for contemporary therapeutic practices related to problemmatic behaviors in regular and special education classrooms, as well as at home, in the clinic, or in the mental hospital.

Briefly, the token economy is a motivational system that requires an individual's adaptive behavior to be reinforced with a concrete event or token that later can be exchanged for a variety of back-up reinforcers. At the outset, the token itself, as a medium of exchange, must be selected. Many different kinds of tokens have been used in the past depending on the age and repertoire of behavior of the individuals, as well as the setting involved (e.g., hospital, clinic, school, home). They have included custom-made coins, points on a tally sheet, plastic credit cards, stamps, coupons, computer cards, and others. The types of tokens used with young and/or special populations have included happy faces, stars, stickers, check marks, points, cards, poker chips, and the like.

This manual describes the use of token and point systems in a distilled form so that practitioners in homes, classrooms, institutions, and communities can quickly grasp the essential elements of a token system and set one up to meet the needs of their own environments.

Teodoro Ayllon, along with Nathan Azrin (one of the authors in this series), pioneered the use of systematic token economies in institutions. Their book, *The Token Economy: A Motivational System for Therapy and Rehabilitation,* remains a classic, the definitive work on the topic. Dr. Ayllon is Professor Emeritus of the Psychology Department at Georgia State University in Atlanta. Dr. Ayllon's other work has been on abnormal behavior in children and behavioral treatment that enlists parents as integral collaborators in the therapeutic enterprise. He is currently finishing a book on child therapy. Dr. Ayllon also maintains an active clinical practice, serving children and adults in Atlanta.

The impact that token systems have as a tool for teaching behavior improvement in a positive way remains one of the major contributions to behavioral psychology. This is especially true in situations where less-structured systems have been ineffective. An important, though often over-looked, dimension of a well-managed token economy is that it not only provides a structure for the person whose behavior it is designed to change, but the system also provides a structure that brings about a profound change in the behavior of the person who manages the token system. It does so in the following ways:

1. It causes the manager to clearly specify both for himself or herself and for the client which behaviors are important to change.

2. It increases the probability that the manager will provide positive consequences for clients who exhibit the appropriate behaviors.

3. It decreases the probability that the manager will resort to negative, coercive procedures in his or her efforts to manage.

4. It increases the likelihood that the manager will be successful in a situation where failure and chaos have been the norm in the past.

This does not mean that token economies are effective for *all* behaviors in *all* situations. Rather, as pointed out in the text, token economies are extremely effective in establishing improved behavior in difficult-to-manage situations.

In summary, *How To Use Token Economy and Point Systems* will provide the reader with a clear road map for using this functional and effective behavioral procedure.

Why a Token Economy?

As caring individuals, we strive to let those around us know when their behavior is appropriate. We truly want them to experience positive consequences for trying to reach a desired goal. However, in trying to meet the many demands placed upon us as parents, teachers, and professionals, it frequently becomes difficult or impossible to provide an immediate "payoff" for an individual's attempt to improve his or her behavior.

For example, parents want to show their son that they appreciate his assuming responsibility for household chores, but they feel they must wait and express their appreciation with an allowance at the first of the month. Teachers want to provide a special privilege for a child who has completed a difficult assignment after many weeks of work. But report cards are months away, and they wish there were other ways to give students daily recognition for their efforts. The psychiatric nurse notices that a patient has made several attempts to communicate with others. She wants to find a way to immediately encourage this behavior but does not know how to do so. She must wait to tell the doctor in her weekly report.

We frequently want to give others rewards for their personal improvement. We know it is important to do so immediately; however, daily demands often make this impossible. What is needed is a bridge between a desired behavior and a reward. There is a way to say "your behavior will be rewarded." This book provides information to assist you in giving such approval through a token system.

The techniques presented in this book are based on years of research conducted in real-life settings. This research has involved parents, teachers, and staff members in institutional environments, and it proved that token and point systems increased skills in children, students, and patients.

The exercises in this book can be used alone or under the direction of a professional who has a background in behavior management. If you master the techniques presented you should be able to more effectively provide immediate positive feedback to those around you, as well as increase their functional living skills.

What Is a Token Economy?

At Home

Charles was an African-American, 13-year-old male, who had been diagnosed as having *conduct disorder* with passive–aggressive features. He often skipped classes because he felt that he was not learning much anyway. His mother had to escort him to school just to be sure that he went. He spent his days and nights watching television and asking his mother for money to buy CDs. He was interested in hip-hop music and fantasized about a job in the music industry. Scoldings from his mother and threats from school personnel brought no changes. The school psychologist suggested that Charles earn his allowance by attending school. He received a daily report from each class he attended. His mother paid him daily for each class. For the first time, Charles earned his allowance just by being in class. His attendance increased, and he was proud to be earning the money instead of nagging his mother and having her put him off. In time, the school psychologist suggested that Charles should have to earn a passing grade in at least two of his classes to receive the same amount of money. Charles was now earning money for his CDs and acquiring skills that would enable him to function as an adult.

In School

Sonny was a fifth-grade student in a suburban elementary school. His intelligence tests and achievement tests indicated that he was very bright and capable, but his performance in class was below his potential. His teachers noticed that he spent much of the class time daydreaming, and he failed to complete daily assignments. Other times he was found drawing pictures of space heroes and building imaginary space capsules. His teachers decided to give Sonny a point for each classroom assignment that he completed with 80% accuracy. Each point was worth 10 minutes to work on a science project that required use of a computer. The points were to be exchanged after lunch each day. Sonny worked to get access to the computer and to be allowed to share his research with the rest of the class during science period. Sonny took pride in sharing his projects with the class. His teachers were pleased with his substantial academic improvement, which allowed him to begin attending the special class for the gifted.

In an Institution

Mary was a 60-year-old, chronic schizophrenic patient in a Midwestern hospital. She had spent 25 years there and had received various treatments, including electroshock therapy and drug therapy—all without success. Lack of interest in self and lack of motivation to interact with others is characteristic of schizophrenic patients. Mary's behavior was typical of those with her diagnosis. She spent most of her time in an unkempt state, just sitting on the side of her bed. Efforts to interest her in self-care, work, and recreation activities had failed.

When a program was established on Mary's ward to pay tokens for getting dressed and communicating with others, she began to do so. Mary gradually learned personal grooming and began to work as a housekeeping assistant. In her job, she interacted with the staff in charge of cleaning and resupplying items as needed. As Mary earned tokens, she exchanged them for new clothes and furnishings for her room. She liked being paid for her performance, and she learned skills that she would be able to use outside the hospital.

These three scenarios illustrate the use of token economies to increase appropriate behavior at home, in school, and in an institution.

Can you think of examples from your own experiences that illustrate the use of token economies?

Defining the Token Economy

A token economy is a motivational system that uses tokens to bridge the delay between a desired behavior and a reward for that behavior. Tokens immediately follow the appropriate behavior and are later exchanged for activities, privileges, or commodities that are rewarding to the individual. Tokens may be plastic chips, stars, stamps, points, stickers, check marks, happy faces, play money, or other distinct units. These items function as rewards by being associated with a "payoff."

Tokens function much the same way as money does in our society. An individual receives a token for a desirable behavior. He or she is given an immediate incentive to repeat the behavior that earned the token. At a later time, tokens are exchanged for self-selected rewards.

List below any items that could be used as tokens in a token economy.

_____

_____

_____

 Exercise 1: Define a Token Economy

What is a token economy? _____

_____

You are on the right track if you said that a token economy is an exchange system in which an individual's positive behavior earns credits that can later be cashed in for a variety of rewards.

List some items that might serve as tokens in your specific setting.

_____

_____

_____

If you are in a school setting you might have selected points, stars, check marks, or a special ink stamp. In the home, you could have used trading stamps, plastic chips from a game, or bottle caps. Institutions would possibly select plastic coins that could be easily carried and yet difficult to duplicate.

Now that you know how a token economy influences the behavior of others, you are ready to learn the basic steps to increase a specific behavior.

▶ **Step 1: Identify Target Behaviors**

It is necessary to focus on one or more positive behaviors that you want to increase. Ask yourself what you want the person to be doing. Be sure to select behaviors that have value in the real world. In defining these behaviors, be specific. Focus on a behavior that you can observe and count. Avoid using vague labels such as "uncooperative," "defiant," or "unmotivated." Pinpoint a positive behavior you want to increase. Think *positively!*

Instead of saying you would "like Sarah to stop being so lazy," indicate constructive behaviors you want Sarah to exhibit. When identifying behaviors, tell *who, what, where,* and *when* (Hall & Hall, 1998b).

Tom and Anne Taylor brought their charming 4-year-old Cindy into family counseling because she refused to sleep through the night in her own room. Each night, she would go to sleep in her bed after a lovely ritual of songs and stories and a glass of water in her favorite cup. Her parents, however, would often be awakened in the middle of the night when she would nudge her mother softly and say, "I had a very bad dream, Mommy. I was all alone and so scared." She would bring her pink and white quilt with her and persuasively say that if she could just sleep on the floor on top of it she would feel safe. This routine had been going on for months and both Tom and Anne were sleep deprived and at their wits' end. They felt that Cindy must have separation anxiety in spite of all their efforts to reassure her that they loved her dearly.

Tom and Anne were asked to define a target behavior. They both said that they wanted Cindy to feel safe enough in her own room to spend the whole night there. The *who, what, where,* and *when* approach was used with Cindy's parents.

Cindy was the *who.*

Remaining in bed was the *what.*

In her room was the *where.*

The *when* was *7 p.m.*

Why is it important to be precise and positive in identifying target behaviors?

_____

_____

 Exercise 2: Identifying Target Behaviors To Increase Their Frequency

In the following examples, identify a target behavior that will earn tokens when a token economy is in effect.

(continues)

At Home

Mark, 13, was often on his dad's last nerve. His dad, Jim, was a "neat freak," and Mark was anything but neat. It seemed to Mark's dad that wherever Mark went he left an endless stream of gum, candy, and potato chip wrappers. This was especially offensive to Jim when it happened in the TV room, because this was a beautifully decorated room where Jim would go to relax. But because of Mark's mess, Jim would end up yelling at Mark every evening when he went into the TV room after dinner. Jim got sick of picking up after Mark, and he also felt angry—and somewhat guilty—that his son was not learning to be responsible and respectful of other people's needs. Something had to change.

What target behavior could Dad identify for Mark?

Who? _____

What? _____

Where? _____

When? _____

Did you identify a specific behavior, such as putting trash in a designated place?

    Yes ☐   No ☐

You might have said that Mark will put his trash in a wastebasket when he came into the TV room. Remember to focus on a specific positive behavior that will enable you to see a change. Dad needs to be able to look in the TV room and observe the results of new behaviors.

In School

Mrs. Robinson enjoyed teaching her fourth graders. She had excellent students, and their grades were good. However, she felt the class could accomplish even more if everyone arrived on time. Ten to fifteen minutes of instruction time was lost each day because students wandered in late. She was tired of waiting for them to get settled so that she could begin with her lesson.

What target behavior could Mrs. Robinson pinpoint for her students?

Who? _____

What? _____

Where? _____

(continues)

When? _____

Did you identify a specific behavior, such as arriving in class on time?

Yes ☐   No ☐

In an Institution

Harley refused to attend the support group meetings for spinal injuries that were held in the rehabilitation unit in a large medical hospital. He spent his days in his room watching television. When others approached him, he pretended to be sleeping. When he had first entered the rehabilitation unit hospital two months before, he had talked to others but he gradually had become nonverbal. The staff was quite concerned and believed that his return to a more normal setting was not likely to occur until he learned to communicate again.

As a staff member of the hospital, what is one target behavior you would like Harley to increase?

Who? _____

What? _____

Where? _____

When? _____

Did you list having Harley talk to others?

Yes ☐   No ☐

Examples of Target Behaviors

At Home

    Complete homework before playing
    Feed animals
    Take out the trash
    Put toys in the toy chest when finished playing
    Clear the table
    Read one hour each night
    Be in bed at the designated time
    Follow instructions without talking back
    Put soiled clothes in the laundry hamper

Wash the dishes
Clear the table after meals
Brush teeth and bathe without assistance
Remain at the table until everyone is finished
Get up and dressed after being called once
Make bed each morning
Mow the lawn once a week
Ask permission to use the car

In School

Complete assignments daily
Be in class on time
Come to class with materials
Raise hand to be recognized
Keep area around desk clean
Obey class rules

In an Institution

Dress self
Make bed
Bathe self
Talk to other patients
Participate in group therapy
Go to the dining room unassisted
Feed self
Write letters
Participate in exercise class
Complete assigned job

Now it is your turn to identify a target behavior that you would like to change in a setting that is important to you.

Who? _____

_____

What? _____

_____

Where? _____

_____

When? _____

_____

Have someone working with you check your work. If you had difficulty, perhaps you selected a situation that was too complex. Begin with a behavior that is easy to identify. Can you define the positive behavior you want to increase? If so, put a check here ☐. If not, review the previous section.

▶ Step 2: Define Tokens

You have now determined which behaviors you want to strengthen. It is time to select an appropriate token of exchange for your particular setting. The following are guidelines that must be followed in the selection of appropriate tokens.

Rule 1: Tokens must be easily available.

Tokens must be objects or symbols readily available to the person administering them. They might include such things as poker chips, plastic coins from a board game, credits in a credit card system, points or checkmarks on a tally sheet, special stamps, or even play money. It is essential that the individual be able to see and count the value of the tokens.

Rule 2: Tokens must be easy to administer.

It is essential for the person delivering tokens to have them handy at all times. One of the principle components of a token economy is that appropriate behavior is reinforced *immediately!* The person dispensing the reinforcement does not have time to search for tokens. They must be available constantly because tokens are the bridge between the time a desired behavior occurs and the reinforcement that follows. The teacher can carry a magic marker in a pocket to place checks on a tally sheet. A mother can carry plastic game chips in her apron. The ward attendant can have imitation coins to give patients wherever they may be. Tokens should not be cumbersome or expensive. They can even be as simple as colored sheets of paper cut in special shapes.

Rule 3: Tokens must be difficult to duplicate by those receiving them.

Tokens, like money, lose their value if they can be counterfeited easily. If you choose to use check marks or stars, you should select colors that are not available to students, children, or patients. Change colors daily. You might want to use your initials on a tally sheet. Handwriting is more difficult to duplicate.

Rule 4: Tokens need to be nontransferable.

Tokens must be of value only in your exchange system.

Rule 5: Keep a record of the tokens earned and spent.

This will provide you with the information you need to determine when to increase or decrease the amount of reinforcement to be most effective.

What can you use to bridge the gap between the desired behavior when it takes place and the reinforcement for it?

_____

_____

A student told his teacher that he would feel more motivated to do his schoolwork if he received his tokens before completing his assignment. What would you suggest the teacher do?

_____

_____

The staff of a psychiatric ward had a problem with a patient who stole tokens from other patients. What would you do?

_____

_____

If you are not sure about your answers, please reread the last section.

Now that you have some basic rules for selecting tokens (currency), try to apply the five rules in the following exercise.

Exercise 3: Selection of Tokens

List items or symbols that could serve as tokens in your particular setting. Remember the five basic rules:

_____

_____

_____

(continues)

I selected these tokens because: _____

_____

_____

If you remembered the five rules, you probably have an effective token. To check yourself, answer the following questions.

1. Was my token easily available? Yes ☐   No ☐

2. Was my token easy to administer? Yes ☐   No ☐

3. Was my token difficult to duplicate? Yes ☐   No ☐

4. Was my token nontransferable? Yes ☐   No ☐

5. Was my token easy to record? Yes ☐   No ☐

▶ **Step 3: Identifying Items, Privileges, and Other Incentives for Rewarding Appropriate Behaviors**

Now that you have identified specific target behaviors and appropriate tokens, it is necessary to determine the payoff for the tokens. This is a critical step. When children, students, and patients receive their tokens they must be exchanged for items or privileges that are truly rewarding. How do you determine which activities or items will increase the desired behaviors?

One effective method for determining what may be motivating to an individual is to observe what the individual chooses to do throughout the day when under no particular demands. There is a high probability that those activities are chosen by an individual as a reward. The English teacher will tell you that his junior high students use any free time to chat together about ball games, movies, and the next big dance. He often rewards his class for working well by letting them have ten minutes of free time at the end of the period. At home, a single parent notices that his twins spend their afternoons watching a particular television show or playing ball with the children next door. On the ward, the day nurse notices Mrs. Jacque spends hours reading movie magazines. Simply observing the activities of persons will give you a good indication of what privileges to plan as rewards for them.

Have you noticed the individuals that you live or work with engaging in activities that you might use as rewards for them? If so, what are they?

_____

_____

Another procedure involves asking the individual to tell you what is personally rewarding. You may want to establish a routine that gives children or residents an opportunity to express their needs. There are numerous ways of providing these opportunities. You might select a definite time each week to interview the individual and let him or her verbally express preferences. An equally effective and less time-consuming procedure is to use a reward questionnaire such as the following.

Reward Questionnaire

Name _____ Date _____

If I could choose any activity or privilege, I would like to do the following:

_____

_____

_____

If I could choose any item that I would like to have for my own, I would want . . . (You may include books, magazines, food, toys, or games.):

_____

_____

_____

_____

You must remember that an event or object may appear to be rewarding to you, but it may not be rewarding to someone else. There is a distinct difference between a reward and a reinforcer. A *reward* may be something you subjectively believe to be pleasing to an individual. A *reinforcer* is an event or item that leads to an *increase* in a desired behavior. It is essential that the reward bring about an increase in the target behavior and, thus, become a reinforcer. Guidelines for selecting rewards tell us to *look* and *listen*. Here are a few exercises to assist you in determining what are effective rewards.

Exercise 4: Selecting Rewards

At Home

Peter had pinpointed a target behavior for Jane, his 3-year-old daughter. He wanted her to take a bath without crying and protesting. He noticed that one of her favorite activities was watching videos, especially *Hercules* and *Aladdin*. He frequently had to drag her screaming away from viewing these videos in order to get her into the bathtub.

By reading the above description of Jane's behavior, what would you suggest as a reward for a peaceful bath time?

_____

_____

If you selected videos as a reward for Jane, you are right.

In School

Osie was a rather shy first grader. He loved reading and playing games on the computer. The teacher had to do very little coaxing to get him involved in either of these activities with his one friend, Andy. His weakness was that he seldom engaged in cooperative play and class projects that required interaction with other children.

If you were Osie's teacher, what rewards could you use to increase the likelihood of more social behavior?

_____

_____

You might let Osie choose a friend to sit with at lunch. Osie could have the opportunity to tell you each day with whom he would like to sit. He may initially choose his friend Andy. Then, perhaps once he begins to interact with others, he may feel comfortable sitting with them. As is true in many cases, in order to find an effective reinforcer, the teacher will have to ask Osie what would be meaningful to him.

In a Work Situation

The management of a manufacturing business instituted a point system to encourage cost-cutting ideas. For every idea that was submitted, 10 points

(continues)

were awarded. For every idea that was used, the 10 points were awarded each month for a year. Management conducted a poll to determine what the workers would like in terms of rewards for which the points could be exchanged. Management was surprised to find that people listed child care, store gift certificates, movie passes, dinners for two, and the like.

Suggest some other practical rewards that might motivate workers. What might the cost for these rewards be in terms of points?

_____

_____

 Exercise 5: Finding Rewards You Can Use

- Observe the individual in your setting throughout the day. Watch what he or she does during free time, and note what activities and items he or she chooses.

- Ask the individual what privileges he or she likes, what items he or she would select to use for a time, or what items he or she would like to own.

- Based upon your observation and your interview, designate one or more rewards for this individual.

Based upon my observation, I think the following activities and items should be appropriate rewards:

_____

_____

Based upon my interview, it appears that the following activities and items would be appropriate rewards:

_____

_____

Are your lists the same? Perhaps not. The true test for determining what is rewarding is to experiment with a wide range of choices and allow the individual to select his or her own payoff. You will learn how to do this in the following section. The list below shows examples of possible rewards.

Sample Rewards

At Home

Television, Nintendo, computer time (in minutes)
Staying up late
Free time
Request for favorite dish
Dessert
A meal at a favorite fast-food restaurant
Going to a movie
Renting a video
Skating
CDs, cassettes
Going to the mall
Time alone with parent
Attend a sporting event
Choice of clothes to wear
Choice of clothes to buy
Guest overnight
Spend the night at home of a friend
Have a friend over for a meal
New toy
Car privileges
Bike privileges

In School

Write on chalkboard
Finger paint
Computer time
Watch a video
Tutor a younger child
Eat with a friend
Extra free time
Sit with the teacher at lunch
Help the librarian, secretary, or custodian
Listen to CDs with headphones
Play a special game
Be the teacher for a lesson
Clean the erasers
Water plants
Operate the slide projector
Be excused from a test

Watch television
Have a popcorn party
Get a "good note" to take home
Be leader of a game
Go to the library
Collect and grade papers

In an Institution

Choice of special foods
Opportunity for privacy
Commissary item such as candy, soft drinks, popcorn, or magazines
Television time
Choice of company at meals
Special clothes
A locked cabinet
Extra time with psychologist or other staff member
Phone calls
Ground privileges
A special chair
Playing cards and board games
Select a job
Visit the barber or beauty shop

Exercise 6: Identifying Rewards To Use in Your Token Economy

List all the activities, items, and privileges you might use in your token economy. Next, think of all the individuals in your setting, and consider what you *see* them doing and *hear* them requesting. Name as many rewards as you can.

I saw them doing: _____

_____

I heard them request: _____

_____

Other items and privileges I have identified: _____

_____

_____

At this point you know how to pinpoint a target behavior, select reinforcing items and activities, and provide a bridge between the two by giving immediate payoff in the form of a token. Now it is essential to learn how to put these components together. The result will be a token economy. To put your system together, ask yourself the following questions:

1. Have I defined target behaviors for the individuals involved?
   Yes ☐   No ☐

2. Have I described these behaviors specifically so that I can observe a change?   Yes ☐   No ☐

3. Have I avoided negative behaviors and concentrated on positive behaviors that I would like to increase?   Yes ☐   No ☐

4. Have I determined activities and privileges that would be reinforcing (rewarding) to the individuals involved?   Yes ☐   No ☐

5. Have I designated tokens (currency) that can be readily available when the individual performs the desired behavior?
   Yes ☐   No ☐

6. Are they easy to administer?   Yes ☐   No ☐

7. Are these tokens difficult to duplicate?   Yes ☐   No ☐

8. Are they nontransferable?   Yes ☐   No ☐

9. Are they easy to record?   Yes ☐   No ☐

If you answered *yes* to all of the questions, you are ready for the fourth step. If you answered *no* to any question, read the section again and perhaps obtain assistance from your instructor or a fellow worker in your setting.

▶ Step 4: Planning an Exchange System

The fourth step is to plan an exchange system for the tokens by doing the following:

1. Specify what performance is required to receive a token or tokens.

2. Make sure that tokens will *immediately* follow the desired response. (This is essential!)

3. Set a value for all privileges and commodities. Individuals must know how many tokens they need to earn their reward.

4. Specify a time and place for the exchange to occur, and decide who will monitor the exchange.

What four things must you do when planning your exchange system?

1. _____

2. _____

3. _____

4. _____

You may have difficulty placing a value on activities and items. The ability to do this comes with practice and through trial and error. One way to determine how much behavior you should require for the payoff is to offer students, children, and patients several items with varying costs. You might want to construct a menu of items and privileges to be purchased with the acquired tokens. Use a wide range of alternatives, and use many variations of a particular reward. If you know Tommy likes candy, have a selection that includes many different kinds of candy. Try to change the reinforcement menu regularly. When an individual has too much of an item, he becomes satiated and bored with it; the item loses its value. For example, you may like spaghetti, but if you eat only spaghetti day after day it loses its appeal. The key is to use *many variations* of the reinforcer. The following examples will assist you in placing values on your rewards and creating your own reinforcement menu.

At Home

Tommy's parents decided to divorce, but they are continuing to co-parent through joint custody. Tommy was an only child who, shortly after entering kindergarten, was described by his teacher as an immature and aggressive boy. He had to be the first to do everything. He pushed and kicked the other boys when he could not get his way.

A meeting was set up to include Tommy; his teacher, Ms. Winner; and both parents. Ms. Winner explained to Tommy that he would get a special sticker for each class period that he could get through without losing his temper. Ms. Winner would fill out a card with the stickers, and Tommy could exchange them for various privileges and prizes in the classroom. For the sake of enhancing Tommy's interest, his parents decided to extend the token system to their respective homes. An identical reinforcement menu was set up in each house. One of his favorite rewards was watching sporting events on TV. Also, he liked playing ball with other kids and getting free toys when he ate out at a particular fast-food restaurant.

It was not long before Tommy was bringing cards home loaded with stickers that he then exchanged for the things he liked. In short order, he had also made friends with the other children in his class.

Tommy's List: Examples of Rewards at Home

Television time (in minutes)
Watching sporting events on TV
Staying up late (in minutes)
Request for favorite dish
Special dessert
A meal at a favorite fast food restaurant
Going to a movie
Renting a video
Going to the park to play ball

Tommy could cash his stickers in each day for rewards or save them for larger rewards. Tommy might choose to cash in three points each night to watch his favorite TV show and save the remaining stickers for a later treat, such as going to a fast-food restaurant. Tommy and his father and mother together decided upon privileges that would be meaningful and realistic. Once Tommy began earning points, he decided to save his points over a period of time for a larger reward, an outing to the park where he could play ball. His parents decided such a trip was worth 16 stickers. This meant that Tommy had to go approximately one week without fighting. Even though the trip to the park was a week away, he was pleased with his *immediate* pay-off of earning stickers daily, and his parents and teacher no longer had to worry about Tommy's behavior.

At School

Mr. Cavallaro was the teacher in charge of the resource room for children who were disruptive and noncompliant in the regular classroom. Most of these children did not finish their class assignments, possibly because they were inattentive and easily provoked into quarrelling and even fighting. He decided to ask the assistance of the school counselor, Ms. Freed. She suggested that the teacher establish a token economy as a motivational tool to increase completion of class assignments. She viewed the students' current inattentiveness and related behaviors as possibly being reinforced by the very attention they commanded from the teacher. Ms. Freed thought that a token economy would also deliver the same attention, but through positive means. Mr. Cavallaro was most interested, so he met with Ms. Freed. Together, they developed the chart shown on page 21 and posted it on the wall for everyone to see.

Each day at 2:00, Mr. Cavallaro checked the students' folders. This took approximately 15 minutes. Students had to earn at least two points to participate. Those with fewer than two points remained at their desks completing work. Students received a ticket with the number of points earned written on it. They wrote their choice of activity below the number and gave it to a monitor who checked to see that they were requesting an activity they had earned. The reinforcement period was the last 30 minutes of the day, a time when students usually finished work and gathered their belongings to prepare for bus call. Mr. Cavallaro changed the menu weekly, sometimes adjusting the point values of the activities as he learned which activities were the most rewarding. The students worked hard to earn their activities at the end of the day. As a result, the entire atmosphere of the class changed. Mr. Cavallaro spent most of his time instructing students and little time disciplining them. He could not believe how his class had changed!

The students helped Mr. Cavallaro operate the token economy. They became competitive about earning points. They also monitored each other's behavior. On Friday afternoons, the students helped Mr. Cavallaro plan the activities for next week's menu. Mr. Cavallaro's token economy was operated at no expense to him. He simply watched to see what activities students enjoyed, asked them to express their priorities, and required that they earn the time to participate.

Point System

At 2:00, I will check each student's work folder and award points for all assignments completed. There are normally eight assignments each day. Students will have the privilege of earning points that will be traded at 2:15.

Task	Point Value
Assignment completed	1
Assignment completed with 80% accuracy or more	2
Points will buy the following at 2:15:	

Reward Menu

Dust erasers	2
Clean chalkboard	2
Water flowers	2
Use watercolors at desk	2
Empty trash	3
Sweep the floor	3
Play with the clay	4
Serve as teacher aide	4

(continues)

Task	Point Value
Go to the library	4
Listen to CDs with headphones	4
Play with puppets	4
Watch television	5
Watch special videos	5
Carry messages	5
Do a science experiment	5
Feed animals in the room	6
Clean the teacher's desk	6
Take the flag down	7
Read stories to younger children	7
Play an electronic game	8
Select any toy at the free-time center	8
Assist the secretary	8
Assist the custodian	8
Give the end of the day report on the intercom	8
Assist the teacher in monitoring the activities	8
A good note home plus free time	8

In an Institution

Gwenn was a 12-year-old with Down syndrome who had spent most of her young life in an institution. She was generally a happy, friendly girl who enjoyed helping the staff with the custodial care of residents who were more profoundly developmentally delayed. She liked to hang around the nurses' station, waiting for an opportunity to play board games with the staff. The one major problem with which the staff wanted help was that Gwenn teased other residents by picking up and hiding the "treats" off their trays (mostly cookies). She caused an uproar at meal and snack times despite all efforts by the staff to discourage her from doing so. Then, someone on the staff read about the power of a token system to change behavior, and suggested they try it. Accordingly, the staff told Gwenn that she would get a token each mealtime she helped out and did not hide food from the residents. She could exchange her tokens for a chance to play a game of checkers or other board games of her choice right after meal or snack time.

The staff also wanted Gwenn to be responsible for her appearance and to acquire job-related skills. Therefore, the staff decided on a list of goals and a reinforcement menu.

Gwenn's Goals

Self-Care

Combs hair. Wears dress, slip, panties, bra, stockings, and shoes (inspection at each mealtime).	1 token
Takes bath at designated time.	1 token
Brushes teeth or gargles at designated time, once daily.	1 token
Participates in exercises conducted by the exercise assistant, twice daily.	1 token
Makes own bed and cleans area around and under bed.	1 token

Meal and Snack Time Aide

Assists in assembling paper napkins and cutlery on counter. Places salt, pepper, and sugar shakers on tables. After the meal (or snack) is over, assists in scraping all leftover food from dishes into garbage bin.	4 tokens

Reinforcement Menu

Choice of board games to play with staff (10 minutes for each game)	5 tokens
Playtime	5 tokens
Walk on hospital grounds (15 minutes)	2 tokens
Consumable items such as candy, cookies, juice, iced tea, or coffee	1–5 tokens

Each week, a staff member met with Gwenn to review her progress and to give her a choice of new, job-related assignments adjusted to her skill repertoire and motivational level.

 Exercise 7: Preparing a Reinforcement Menu

- Think of items and activities that you could give in exchange for tokens.
- List all the possible items and activities.
- Assign a value to each.
- Decide upon a time and place for your token exchange.
- Determine who will monitor this exchange.

(continues)

Tokens may be traded for the following: Value

_____   _____

_____   _____

_____   _____

_____   _____

_____   _____

_____   _____

_____   _____

_____   _____

Tokens will be exchanged at the following time(s):

_____

_____

The place for exchange is: _____

_____

_____

The individual who will monitor the exchange is:

_____

_____

Points To Remember

Lessen Requirements If Necessary

Adjust your requirements so that it is possible for everyone to earn a token. You may have to begin with a small portion of the desired behavior. You can gradually increase the amount of behavior necessary to earn a token.

At Home

Mrs. Kalabash wanted Selena, her 8-year-old daughter, to clean up her room, which was a "disaster area." Her toys were scattered all over the floor and so were her dirty clothes! Mrs. Kalabash knew that she must not require too much at first, or Selena would give up. Instead of having Selena earn points for cleaning her room, she began by concentrating on picking up items of dirty clothing from the floor and putting them in a hamper in the closet. After Selena began earning points for this target behavior, Mrs. Kalabash added the additional requirement of picking up toys.

In School

Coach Seferino wanted Mario to practice making a basket from the free throw line. But Mario was easily distracted by the girls practicing their cheer-leading routines next to the stands. The coach knew that Mario needed a lot of reassurance and positive reinforcement. Unfortunately, it was hard to reinforce him because much of his attention was focused on the cheerleaders' practice rather than the coach's instructions.

The coach decided to focus on one rule for Mario to achieve in his class. He knew that Mario was good at following directions, so he gave Mario a point each time he made a basket during a 15-minute period of practice. When Mario earned a designated number of points, he could trade his points for a short breather—which in Mario's case meant taking a 5-minute break to watch the cheerleading squad. When Mario mastered that goal, the coach added an additional basketball-related skill.

In an Institution

The ward staff was concerned because Don would communicate with only one person on the staff. The staff's goal was to have him communicate his needs to any ward staff member. Realizing this long-range goal was unachievable immediately, they decided to administer tokens for eye contact. Every time Don looked at the person speaking to him, he received a token and verbal praise. The first few times, the attendant had to gently move Don's head so that he was looking at him. Once Don began earning tokens for looking at the person talking to him, he was also required to nod. Later still, a "yes " or "no" to questions was expected in order for him to receive tokens.

Administer Tokens Immediately After the Desired Response

At Home

Mrs. Pearson wanted Jenny-Greer, her cute 2-year-old, to sit for supper with the family. Whenever Mrs. Pearson observed Jenny-Greer doing this, she gave her a plastic chip that she could later trade to watch her favorite video or do other fun activities.

In School

Mr. Meister wanted Cymbal to clean up around her desk. Cymbal made good grades, but she could not keep her school supplies organized in the proper place. Whenever Mr. Meister saw Cymbal picking up books, paper, and other supplies he gave her a check mark on her tally sheet. She traded these at the end of the day for a special game.

In an Institution

Rosa liked to read the latest news in the *Enquirer*. She also liked to start arguments with the other residents in the nursing home. The aide wanted Rosa to be friendly and talk with the others in a positive manner. Whenever she observed Rosa talking with other patients without arguing, she gave her a token to be traded in for her favorite tabloid.

Reinforcers Given Only with Tokens

Activities and commodities used as reinforcers must be made available only through tokens. They should not be free.

At Home

Mrs. Albert could not understand why Melisha had stopped earning points for a special afternoon snack. After talking with the mother of Melisha's friend down the street, she realized what had happened. Melisha was stopping by her friend's house on the way home from school. There she enjoyed a snack that was free!

In School

The English teacher at a middle school attempted to establish a token economy. Students received points for work completed. These points could be exchanged for candy. But something was wrong! Few students earned the required points. The English teacher knew the students liked candy, for he found candy wrappers on the floor and in the trash can. Then he realized that the students did not have to earn candy. They brought it to school in their pockets!

In an Institution

Billy was an adolescent boy in a psychiatric hospital that ran on a token system. According to the staff, he was not motivated to earn the tokens. His parents brought him money, which he spent on the same items for which the tokens could be exchanged. The staff solved the problem by opening a bank account for Billy and setting a limit on bank withdrawals. Each week, in exchange for a specific number of tokens, he could withdraw $5.00. This meant that Billy still needed to earn tokens in order to gain access to his bank account.

Points To Consider If Problems Occur

Problems may arise in establishing a token economy. However, if you know how to handle them in advance, they are easily overcome.

1. **Did you provide tokens during or immediately following the desired behavior? Yes ☐ No ☐**

Remember that tokens enable you to provide reinforcement *immediately*. In order to obtain an increase in behavior, frequent reinforcement is necessary until the desired level is reached.

2. **How are you maintaining your token economy?**

To maintain a token economy, two points must be considered. First, it is essential to adjust the reinforcement menu periodically. Items and privileges should be varied to prevent satiation or boredom. Second, the number of tokens required to earn items may need to be altered from time to time. For example, an individual may earn enough tokens to get the desired reward and then quit. This situation may be caused by too low a value on the reinforcers (they are too easy to earn). By increasing the cost of popular items, more tokens will be required to earn them. You may also find that an individual's behavior improves when he or she is not earning sufficient tokens to purchase desired items. In order to maintain this improvement, you will need to decrease the token value of target behaviors or increase the cost of items on the menu.

3. **What do you do if an individual indicates he will not participate in the token system?**

This is less likely to occur if the persons earning the tokens have some responsibility in setting up the token economy. Participants may assist in selecting the reinforcers available for the token exchange. Research indicates that those who initially protest will participate once they begin earning rewards or observe others doing so. The best strategy is to proceed with the system and ignore the verbal behavior of those who protest. Their behavior will most likely change when they see that the only way to obtain highly desired privileges and activities is by earning tokens.

4. What if your token system is too costly to administer in terms of time and effort?

In most instances, the simpler the token system, the more successful it is likely to be. When possible, plan a system that enables individual participants to assist with the management. Some token economies can be run entirely by the students. Ayllon and Azrin (1968b) had patients operate the concession stand. Individuals can use tokens to purchase privileges that are a part of the system. They can dispense tokens, set up reinforcement activities, and monitor the exchange of tokens for reinforcers.

5. How do you gain the interest and participation of persons who are not interested in rewards or severely handicapped?

It may be necessary to use reinforcement samples to get your token economy going when an individual has had limited contact with the available reinforcers. Ayllon and Azrin (1968a) let patients, who would not pay tokens to watch a movie, sample a free movie. Movies then became a favorite item on the reinforcement menu. With severely handicapped persons, it may be necessary to physically prompt the desired behavior, present the token, and then immediately carry out the exchange. Once this chain of events has been established, the time between earning the token and the exchange for the reinforcer can gradually be lengthened.

6. How do you fade out the token system?

Token systems should be modified or faded out once the desired behaviors have become a regular part of the person's repertoire and are being maintained by more natural consequences for good performance. For example, one parent who had established a token system with her three young children reported that she was still using the system four years later, although the behaviors and reinforcers had changed dramatically and the system was almost entirely self-administered by the children.

One way of fading the token system is to gradually delay the opportunity for exchange. Phillips (1968), in the Teaching Family Program for predelinquent adolescents, faded residents from the token system by shifting from a daily earning of privileges to a weekly earning of privileges to an honor system in which no token exchange was used if appropriate behavior was maintained at an acceptable level.

Pairing social reinforcers with the delivery of tokens is also important if behaviors are to be maintained in natural settings. Delivery of the token should be accompanied by a statement praising a specific behavior. For example, you might say, "Here is a token for completing your assignment," or give a smile, a pat on the back, or other social reinforcer.

Selecting items and privileges that are likely to occur in a variety of settings also makes it easier to shift away from a token system. The reinforcement menu may initially have trinkets and tangible items that have fixed prices. When more activities and privileges are included in the menu, these are likely to occur as a natural payoff in a number of settings. For more information on selecting reinforcers, see *How to Select Reinforcers,* by Hall and Hall (1998).

Review

Plan your own token economy by following these steps:

1. Identify target behavior(s). _____

   _____

   _____

2. Designate backup reinforcers (activities, items, food).

   _____

   _____

3. Describe your medium of exchange. What will you use as tokens?

   _____

   _____

4. Establish a value for your reinforcers. How much behavior will be required for each?

   _____

   _____

   _____

   _____

   _____

   _____

   _____

(continues)

5. Who will administer the tokens? _____

_____

_____

6. When and where will the exchange(s) of tokens for reinforcers take place?

_____

_____

7. Who will monitor the exchange? _____

_____

_____

References and Further Reading

Alber, S. R., & Heward, H. L. (1996). "Gotcha!" Twenty-five behavior traps guaranteed to extend your students' academic and social skills. *Intervention in School and Clinic, 31*(5), 285–289.

Alberto, P. A., & Troutman, A. C. (1990). *Applied behavior analysis for teachers: Influencing student performance* (3rd ed.). Columbus, OH: Charles E. Merril.

Ayllon, T., & Azrin, N. (1965). The measurement and reinforcement of behavior of psychotics. *Journal of Experimental Analysis of Behavior, 8,* 357–383.

Ayllon, T., & Azrin, N. (1968a). Reinforcer sampling: A technique for increasing the behavior of mental patients. *Journal of Applied Behavior Analysis, 1,* 13–20.

Ayllon, T., & Azrin, N. (1968b). *The token economy: A motivational system for therapy and rehabilitation.* New York: Appleton-Century-Crofts.

Ayllon, T., Garber, S., & Allison, M. (1977). Behavioral treatment of childhood neurosis. *Psychiatry, 40,* 315–322.

Ayllon, T., Garber, S., & Pisor, K. (1975). The elimination of discipline problems through a combined school–home motivational system. *Behavior Therapy, 6,* 616–626.

Ayllon, T., Layman, D., & Burke, S. (1972). Disruptive behavior and reinforcement of academic performance. *The Psychological Record, 22,* 315–323.

Ayllon, T., Layman, D., & Kandel, H. (1975). A behavioral educational alternative to drug control of hyperactive children. *The Journal of Applied Behavior Analysis, 8,* 137–146.

Ayllon, T. & Roberts, M. D. (1974). Eliminating discipline problems by strengthening academic performance. *The Journal of Applied Behavior Analysis, 7,* 71–76.

Ayllon, T. & Rosenbaum, M. (1977). The behavioral treatment of disruption and hyperactivity in school settings. In B. Lahey and A. Kazdin (Eds.), *Advances in Child Clinical Psychology* (pp. 83–118). New York: Plenum.

Ayllon, T., Smith, D., & Rogers, W. (1970). Behavior management of school phobia. *Journal of Behavior Therapy and Experimental Psychiatry, 1,* 125–138.

Hall, R. V., & Hall, M. L. (1998a). *How to select reinforcers* (2nd ed.). Austin, TX: PRO-ED.

Hall, R. V., & Hall, M. L. (1998b). *How to use systematic attention and approval.* (2nd ed.). Austin, TX: PRO-ED.

Glynn, S. M. (1990). Token economy approaches for psychiatric patients: Progress and pitfalls over 25 years. *Behavior Modification, 14,* 383–407.

Jackson, N. C., & Mathews, R. M. (1995). Using public posting to increase contributions to a multipurpose senior center. *Journal of Applied Behavior Analysis, 28,* 449–455.

Miller, D. L., & Kelly, M. L. (1994). The use of goal setting and contingency contracting for improving children's homework performance. *Journal of Applied Behavior Analysis, 27,* 73–84.

Paul, G., Stuve, P., & Menditto, A. (1997). Social-learning program (with token economy) for adult psychiatric patients. *The Clinical Psychologist, 50*(1), 14–17.

Phillips, E. L. (1968). Achievement place: Token reinforcement procedures in a home-style reha-bilitation setting for predelinquent boys. *Journal of Applied Behavior Analysis, 1,* 213–223.

Staub, R. W. (1990). The effects of publicly posted feedback on middle school students' disrup-tive hallway behavior. *Education and Treatment of Children, 13,* 249–257.

Sullivan, M. A., & O'Leary, S. G. (1990). Maintenance following reward and cost token programs. *Behavior Therapy, 21,* 131–149.

Wolf, M. M., Giles, D. K., & Hall, R. V. (1968). Experiments with token reinforcement in a reme-dial classroom. *Behavior Research and Therapy, 6,* 51–64.